Praise for
Aspire to Be Inspired

Keith Carlson's latest book, *Aspire to Be Inspired,* captures the spirit of nursing and highlights the tremendous value nurses possess. With multiple perspectives, Keith gives voice to empowering nurses to take their knowledge and experience and express it in work they love. The section "Your Nursing Career and a Latte" beautifully describes the development of our nursing journey and left me wanting to read more.

For nurses that feel stuck or wish to take their careers to the next level, Nurse Keith can help and this book is for you!

Michelle Podlesni, RN
President, National Nurses in Business Association
www.nnbanow.com
www.unconventionalnurse.com

You deserve to thrive in your career, and Keith Carlson is determined to help you do it. *Aspire to be Inspired* is rich with wisdom, support, and hope – all to help you become your best self while finding joy and meaning in your work. There is take-home value on every single page!

Beth Boynton, RN, MS
www.confidentvoices.com

Keith Carlson is an artist. Through prose and metaphor, he interweaves his professional experience as a nurse and his gift of writing, inspiring nurses to live their unique rhythmic expression in the world of healthcare.

A brilliant storyteller, Keith's words coax the imagination, guiding nurses on an exciting journey, igniting the passionate spark of creativity for nurses to serve not only as advocates for their joy, but to courageously bring their innovative ideas to the table towards positive social change.

Keith's wisdom reawakens the nursing profession's caring and compassionate calling, grounding nurses to connect with their purpose, meaning, and artistry within the vocation of nursing. His pioneering work inspires nurses around the world to live their soul calling.

Caroline Pauline Cárdenas, RN, MSN, CBCN, RYT 200hr
Embodied Movement Meditation Educator & Nurse Educator
Creator of The Hula Hoop Girl & Producer of Hawaii
Hoopdance Retreat
www.TheHulaHoopGirl.com

In this inspiring book, Keith offers nurses the chance to prove the old adage that "no man is an island"—or more specifically, that no nurse stands alone.

In the age of professional and personal coaching and mentoring, Keith opens a window of opportunity for all who seek solace and support in times of significant uncertainty.

Keith knows that we all need each other, and it is that sense of collaboration and unity that can change the healthcare system from the inside out.

I invite you to find inspiration and strength in Keith's thoughtful essays.

Betty Noyes, RN, BSN, MA
President, Noyes & Associates, Ltd.
www.noyesconsult.com

When you sit down to read Keith Carlson's new book, *Aspire To Be Inspired*, it's like opening a box of mixed chocolates. Each chapter is served up like a delicious portion in a reader's buffet of options. First, they're bite-size, each chapter no more than a few pages. Second, they're all different, so you won't get bored of one taste; some are piquant, some sweet, and others you might need to spend more time chewing.

No worries if you're a vegan or have food allergies. If you're a nurse, these chapter-sized bites are sure to please any palate. I dare you to eat just one.

Warning: They're a little addictive.

Candy Campbell, DNP, RN, CNL, FNAP
Best-selling author, award winning actor, and filmmaker
www.candycampbell.com

This is a great book for nurses to get in the right mindset at the beginning of their career. Keith poses important questions that enable the new nurse to begin on the right foot.

Keith speaks like that wise, experienced nurse on the unit who is your biggest cheerleader, but also holds you to a high standard; the nurse who makes you want to be better for not only them, but yourself as well. He verbalizes concepts that are essential to understand but difficult to articulate early in your nursing career. Being aware of these things from the beginning can save nurses a lot of frustration, heartache, and disappointment.

I highly recommend this book for new nurses. This should be required reading for students in their final semester of nursing school!

Kati Kleber, BSN RN CCRN

www.freshrn.com

The next best thing to having the authentic and genuine Keith in person as a coach is reading his words.

This book is so relatable, but best of all it's a gift of inspiration. For me, it's like a refreshing dip in a cool and secluded lake deep in the forest and remembering what's important – who I am as a nurse and a person.

Thank you, Keith, for the much needed focus.

Beth Hawkes, MSN, RN-BC

Nursing Professional Development Specialist

http://nursecode.com

Volume Two

Aspire to be Inspired

Creating a
Nursing Career
That Matters

Keith Carlson
RN, BSN, NC-BC

Nurse Keith
Coaching

Santa Fe, New Mexico

NURSE KEITH CAREER MASTERY SERIES

Published by: Nurse Keith Coaching
           57 Calle Francisca
           Santa Fe, NM, 87507-0150
           NurseKeith.com

Editors: Jeffrey Braucher, Mary Rives
Book design and production: Ann Lowe

Printed in the United States of America

This book is dedicated to nurses everywhere.
Whether you're already inspired or seeking inspiration,
this is for you.

Contents

Acknowledgments & Gratitude

M
Y IMMENSE and ongoing gratitude and love to Mary Rives, wife and business partner extraordinaire. She's the essential fuel that keeps my engine happily humming.

Much love to Rene Rives, my amazing son who walks this earth with a compassionate heart and the kind presence of a true gentleman. Much love as well to Bevin Shagoury, my beloved daughter-in-law, whose support and caring are like a balm for this nurse's soul.

A bow of thanks to Jeffrey Braucher, "The Santa Fe Word Doctor," for flawless editing and proofreading.

Deep gratitude to Ann Lowe, my stalwart and talented book designer.

Many thanks to Michelle Podlesni, Candy Campbell, Betty Noyes, Beth Boynton, Beth Hawkes, and Kati Kleber for their friendship and support.

Special recognition to Renee Thompson, Caroline Cardenas, and Kim Allen for being extraordinary nurse friends whose empathy and presence are beyond measure.

Ongoing gratitude to Kevin Ross, Elizabeth Scala, Sean Dent, and Ashley Pofit Miller for their support and camaraderie in the RNFM Radio/Pulse Media family of like-minded nurses.

Special thanks to you, the all-important reader. Without you, a book is just a bunch of words with no audience to imbibe them.

Preface

WHILE CONSIDERING the subject of the second book in the Nurse Keith Career Mastery Series, I felt strongly that a book was needed that would be a collection of inspiring essays for nurses in need of a proverbial shot in the arm vis-à-vis their careers. Nursing can be a lonely business, and we can all use something to lift our spirits from time to time.

We nurses can get pretty crusty and crispy in the course of our careers, and a little inspiration can go a long way. Equally, nursing students and prenursing students can feel confused and uninspired as they submit themselves to the rigors of their nursing education and professional indoctrination.

I began writing my blog, Digital Doorway, back in January of 2005. At that time, blogging was relatively new, and most of us had no idea what we were doing. As the blog developed, I noticed that the more I wrote about my nursing career and the healthcare industry, the more followers and notoriety I gained.

Writing about nursing hit a nerve, and I've continued in that vein for years, writing for Digital Doorway, as well as a variety of nursing and healthcare websites, books, and print publications. Meanwhile, podcasting has become another medium through which I reach an audience hungry for information, education, inspiration, and entertainment.

While my writing and podcasting do indeed delve into advice and instruction regarding what I call the nursing career toolbox (e.g., resumes, cover letters, etc.), one of my happy places as a writer lies in the realm of inspiration. My inspirational writing isn't necessarily in the *Chicken Soup For The Soul* genre, but likely gets the same job done from a different stylistic viewpoint.

In my work as a nurse writer, blogger, career coach, podcaster, speaker, and consultant, I strive to fulfill my mission of inspiring nurses to find the professional joy and power within their careers that they deserve to experience. Similarly, I seek to bolster and embolden those who are not yet nurses but who feel a calling to join our ranks.

It's often said that nurses are the backbone and connective tissue of health care worldwide. While I agree with that assertion, I can also make an argument for nurses being the heart and lifeblood of health care, not to mention the very mitochondria that drive the healthcare engine.

This book is about being who you are as a nurse and finding a way to create the life and career you want. It's less about action and more about your mind, but you may indeed be spurred into action by what you encounter herein.

Read this book in whatever way works for you. Each essay stands on its own, so there's no reason to read it from cover to cover. Open it randomly whenever you want some inspiration, or search the table of contents for a subject that catches your eye at just the right moment.

This collection of essays is meant to be a dose of medicine for the soul, spirit, and heart of the nurses who read it. It is a love letter from my nurse's heart to yours.

May you be inspired.

Keith Carlson
Santa Fe, New Mexico

Foreword

AROUND 2011, I first came to know Keith Carlson as @ nursekeith on Twitter, and I actually didn't know his last name until I started reading his blog, Digital Doorway. It's funny that I didn't realize at first that they were the same person! Keith and I became instant friends. Why? Because there was something about Keith that drew me to his writing, his calm yet powerful message, and who he is as a human being.

Keith has a way of gently encouraging nurses to think beyond the traditional "that's the way we've always done things" to the more introspective and personal, "I can be and do anything I want as a nurse". I find that his writing helps me to feel centered, and I can see his profound impact on other nurses, especially those struggling with their careers.

I've been a nurse for 27 years and have done almost everything you can do, from bedside nursing, homecare, and managed care to unit manager, educator, executive, and now a successful nurse entrepreneur. I've met and spoken to thousands of nurses over the years about why they chose this profession, what it means to be a nurse, and how to articulate their value to other members of the healthcare team and the public at large. What I know in my heart is that nurses at all levels need help. Nurses need support and guidance from those of us who have walked the same path and worn similar shoes.

The way nurses practice has changed dramatically over the years. It wasn't that long ago that nurses were viewed simply as handmaidens to physicians. They regularly gave up their chairs to the all-powerful doctors and didn't carry stethoscopes. At that time, nursing was considered a passive occupation and viewed as a non-professional service position. A job description in the early 1900's included expectations such as maintaining a warm temperature in patient rooms and mopping floors.

Today, a nurse's job description includes advanced disease-specific assessments, use of sophisticated equipment, as well as diagnosing and writing prescriptions in the context of advanced practice. Moreover, nurses need to fully comprehend research, regulatory requirements, and the financial implications of healthcare.

When teaching a clinical course, I frequently find myself saying, "back in the day…" or using the phrase, "old school" to describe how we used to do things. Although the technology has changed (who remembers paper charting and counting drips on our IVs?), the heart and spirit of the nurse has not. Nursing is about making a difference in the lives of others, no matter the role you assume, where you practice, or what technology is available.

In his new book, *Aspire to Be Inspired*, Keith reminds us that having a successful nursing career is about each one of us taking the helm of our practice and not passively allowing others to determine our future. We each have the ability to create an individualized and unique nursing career based on what's important to us, rather than on a preconceived notion of what it means to be a nurse.

In his books, blogs, and podcasts, Keith guides nurses down the path of crafting a meaningful and sustainable nursing career for life. It's nice to know that Keith is always there, and that he continues to provide nurses with the inspiration and insight they need to be successful.

As Keith so eloquently stated (with a nod to the poet Mary Oliver), "*Tell me, what is it you plan to do with your one wild and precious career?*" In his new book, Keith provides both novice and seasoned nurses with a foundation from which to answer this and many other important questions. Be prepared to be inspired!

Renee Thompson, DNP, RN, CMSRN
www.reneethompsonspeaks.com

Introduction

IMAGINE THAT you've been a nurse for 18 years and things have been more or less humming along. However, there's a nagging feeling at the back of your mind that something isn't quite right. You don't know what it is, but you acknowledge it's there and it's growing.

At this point in your career, you don't want help with your resume or interview skills—that's not where the lack is felt. Rather, you need an infusion of inspiration, some words of wisdom or encouragement to keep you working toward your most optimal life and satisfying career trajectory.

Or let's imagine that you're a new nurse with a few years of experience. You've been appropriately focused on skills mastery since graduating from nursing school and beginning your first real job in acute care, but you know there's more to this nursing stuff than PICC lines and physical assessment. Now that you've found your stride, you need to get inspired again about why you became a nurse in the first place. You need to elevate to the next level in your career.

Nursing is historically a task-based profession. In fact, our professionalization is still an ongoing process, and we've made great strides since the days when we were essentially the servants of all-knowing physicians. We're no longer simple gophers who do doctors' biddings; we're highly respected professionals with the wherewithal and acumen to directly impact patients' lives in myriad ways. We aren't just the doers of tasks; we are scientists, educators, researchers, leaders, autonomous advanced-practice healthcare providers, executives, and entrepreneurs.

If we're not careful, the work of nursing can become robotic and habitual. We stop seeing the patient in room 202 and instead see only the diagnosis and the tasks at hand. Nursing is so much more than that, but we can feel beaten down to the point where we just soldier on, even as we lose touch with what got us to the bedside in the first place.

Nurses need inspiration that can put them back in touch with what makes them tick. There's plenty of science in nursing, and there's plenty of heart and soul as well. This book is about the heart and soul—may you feel its impact in the pages that follow.

CHAPTER 1

A Message to the Nurse's Future Self

SO, NURSE, it's twenty years in the future, and you now have two more decades of nursing under your belt. You've cared for thousands of patients, held thousands of hands, and looked into thousands of pairs of eyes. What do you remember, and what do your patients recall? What stands out for you? How does your career compare to your expectations, dreams, and aspirations?

What do your patients remember about you? They don't usually remember your name. Most of them instead recall how you cared for them and touched their lives at a vulnerable and frightening time.

Next, they usually remember your kindness, the way you looked at them, fluffed their pillow, started an IV with extra care, or made them more at ease. They may not recall exact moments, but they might say, "You know, when I was in the hospital in 2014, there was this nurse who was so kind to me. I can't remember who he was, but he really made my hospitalization so much gentler. I wish I could remember his name so I could send him a note. God bless that man."

I've actually heard people say things like this. Have you? Do you think they say things like this about you? I sure hope they do.

Nurses Remember

So, future nurse, what do the last twenty years of nursing look like to you? How do you feel about your career? Did you burn out or did you burn bright? Did you care well or did you end up no longer caring at all?

What do you remember? Do you remember the kindness of your colleagues, or the way they bullied one another? If you witnessed bullying, do you recall stepping in to interrupt the harassment, or did you look the other way? Did you speak up, or was your very silence an act of complicity? Will you remember standing up to injustice or turning your back when your voice was needed most?

Did nursing over the last twenty years build you up or tear you down? Was your spirit lifted by your work or diminished by it? Did your body suffer from the stress of your work, or did you care for yourself well enough to survive, and possibly even thrive?

When you think about your patients, do you think of them with caring and compassion, or do you think of them as weighty burdens on your nurse's soul?

When you think about your colleagues, were they a source of support or a source of complaints, rancor, and resentment? How did you support one another? How did you make it through the tough times? Did you laugh? Did you cry? Were hugs readily available? Was mutual support part and parcel of your day?

The Future You Desire

In thinking about how you will look back on your career, is there anything you would like to change now in order to make that future brighter?

Do some of the questions I've asked make you feel uncomfortable? Do you recognize ways in which nursing has already become burdensome? Are there ways in which you may already be burning out? Are your colleagues also suffering? Have you turned your backs on one another already, or are you there for each other through thick and thin?

If you think about what you will feel and experience in twenty years as you look back on your career, what can you do now to alter that potential future outcome? How can you approach your work, your colleagues, your patients, and your career in a way that will make you reminisce with pride, joy, health intact, compassion, and fulfillment?

Think hard, and consider the future you desire, and then consider how to make that future a reality by acting righteously and authentically in the present moment.

Nurse, the future is yours to create. How will you create a great one?

CHAPTER 2

Be Yourself,
Everyone Else Is Already Taken

OWNING and stepping into your own genius as a nurse is important, and genius is, of course, relative for all nurses.

At times we can lose heart and feel that we just can't become the person or professional we thought we could be. However, seeking our own individual path is paramount when it comes to creating a career that feels tailor-made just for us, not just a path someone else said was the best one to follow.

Whether you feel like an impostor or your career has grown stale, there's nothing you can be other than yourself. And if you're trying terribly hard to be just like someone else (or do what others tell you is right), you may end up missing the mark altogether.

Oscar Had It Right

When Oscar Wilde said, "Be yourself, everyone else is already taken," he wasn't kidding. If you haven't read any Wilde since high school, you might want to revisit his work or find one of the many movies or books about his life. But simply taking this excellent advice to heart will be enough to potentially imbue your life and nursing career with a more solid sense of self *a la Wilde*.

Emulate, But Don't Ruminate

Many of us have mentors or people we look up to. A role model is a wonderful person to have in your life, but when we fall into negative rumination about our own shortcomings in comparison to our role models, we can get into trouble.

Comparing ourselves to others is a double-edged sword. The comparison can sometimes galvanize us into inspired action and forward movement, but if we instead fall into despair by comparing ourselves with our heroes, we can devolve into rumination, self-doubt, and a cessation of progress in the right direction.

We can emulate others we admire, and we can even attempt to duplicate the steps they took in order to achieve success. However, we must watch for the trap of comparing ourselves from a negative vantage point that may cause us to feel discouraged by the steep climb ahead.

Believing that our role model is luckier, smarter, more attractive, or just plain old better than we are is a trap. If you're in that kind of headspace right now, there's no better time than right now to stop that line of thinking.

It's All Relative

We all have our own areas of strength and expertise, and none is better than the other. We need to own our genius, internalize our own merit, and create a personal brand that's emboldened by what makes us unique.

Nursing can sometimes feel like it's made up of silos that are unequal in value (e.g., school nurse vs. ICU nurse). We have to push back against the notion that a nurse who cares for the critically ill has more relative value than a nurse who monitors students' medical conditions closely enough so that they can participate fully in their education. It's the old conundrum of comparing apples to oranges.

If we can accept our own worth, we can begin to believe that our own unique career path has merit.

The Iconoclast Nurse

An iconoclast can be defined as a person who goes against the grain, rebels against convention, or otherwise subverts the dominant paradigm in the interest of marching to the beat of his or her own drum. Picasso was assuredly an iconoclast, and there are plenty more to choose from in the arts, sciences, and other disciplines.

When I graduated from nursing school in 1996, I announced to my classmates and professors that I was not going to pursue a med-surg position; rather, I was choosing to sink my teeth into nursing at an inner city community health center providing comprehensive care to under-served populations.

I was told that not seeking an acute care entry-level nursing position was professional suicide, and that my career would be doomed from the start. Needless to say, I rejected all such opinions, took the health center position, and created a career that was completely removed from acute care and the world of hospitals. That was an iconoclastic career move, and I've never looked back.

Making the Choice

You may have a very distinctive and out-of-the-box vision for your nursing career. Whether you're just out of school or preparing for a mid-career shift or retirement, you may indeed make a choice that throws your colleagues for a loop and makes them question your sanity.

Oscar Wilde would have a field day convincing you about your worth and the value of being yourself. Sadly, he's not around, so unless you want to get out the Ouija board, you might as well heed his simple but deep advice and cajole yourself to follow your bliss.

Nurse entrepreneurs can feel like they're out on a limb starting businesses when their friends are in the ICU or ER. New nurses can feel profound self-doubt when they choose not to take the tried and true route of med-surg (even when there are no med-surg jobs to be had). And a mid-career nurse ready for a major change may also receive feedback that she's throwing it all away for a pipe dream when she should just be happy where she is.

Iconoclasts and those of us who write our own career scripts must develop thick skins, powerful bullshit detectors, and the ability to forge ahead based on our own innate wisdom and inner compass. Sure, we may sometimes fall on our faces or fail miserably, but staying in a silo just because everyone else says you should isn't necessarily the life and career many of us dreamed of.

Making a choice to change lanes or abandon the highway altogether isn't easy, and you'll suffer some flat tires and empty gas tanks for doing so. But you know, Oscar Wilde and Pablo Picasso did it, and so can you.

So be yourself, nurses; everyone else is indeed already taken.

CHAPTER 3

Your Wild and Precious Nursing Career

ANY TIME WE REFLECT on our lives in order to move forward, we have the opportunity to assess many of its aspects.

The poet Mary Oliver once wrote in her poem "The Summer Day:"

> *Tell me, what is it you plan to do*
> *with your one wild and precious life?*

Taking Oliver's poem fragment as a place to begin, I'll ask this question:

> *Tell me, what is it you plan to do*
> *with your one wild and precious career?*

Your nursing career can be populated with a plethora of mixed emotions, including excitement, joy, trepidation, remorse, regret, and expectation. Your emotions may run high at the holidays, your birthday, or the New Year, but any moment can be auspicious for self-reflection and planning for the future.

Resolutions vs. Intentions

I'm never one to make resolutions (since they're so easily broken). Instead, I set intentions, because intentions are simply the verbalization of one's desires, not a sacrosanct promise. This may seem like splitting hairs, but the distinction helps me to feel empowered by my goals and desires, rather than weighed down by their apparent impossibility.

Taking into consideration various aspects of your career, how would you intend to do things differently in the year to come? What intentions can you set for yourself in terms of reduced stress, improved satisfaction, stronger skills, or better relationships with colleagues and patients? What other areas are crying out for your attention—and intention?

Seize the Day

There's no time like the present to set the intention of a more satisfying career and set some important wheels in motion.

- What indeed do you plan to do with your wild and precious nursing career?
- What do you want?
- Where would you like to go?
- Who would you like to collaborate with?
- How would you like to feel at work?
- Who would you truly like to be?

These and other questions are crucial to answer as you set intentions to manifest your dreams, desires, and goals.

The 10,000-Foot View

WHEN CONTEMPLATING your career, you need to consider a lot of detail: your resume, cover letters, thank-you letters, LinkedIn profile, interview skills, the employers you're interested in contacting, etc. These details can feel overwhelming, and you need to tackle them one at a time with a systematic approach. Breaking it all down into digestible discrete tasks is a great way to go about it. Otherwise, the breadth and depth of your career to-do list can feel like too much of an uphill battle that even Sisyphus would consider avoiding.

For some, the details are a comfort. One day you tackle the resume; the next you make sure your cover letter is flawless. And the rest of the week you begin filling out the new job search spreadsheet you created to track your applications. It's a very personal journey and process.

The Big Picture

While you may or may not be enjoying your slog through the details, you also need to periodically remove yourself from them and consider the big picture, often referred to as "the 10,000-foot view."

The big picture of our career and professional trajectory doesn't necessarily avoid things like resumes and job applications, but it does consider the broader agenda, including short- and long-term considerations.

The 10,000-foot view examines where you've been over the arc of your career, where you currently are, and where you may want to go, no matter how circuitous or confusing the potential path (or paths) may appear.

From this larger perspective, you don't just ponder how much you like or dislike your current job or area of nursing specialization. Rather, you examine:

- Where you'd like to be in two years, five years, ten years, or beyond
- Your level of satisfaction with your career so far
- The overarching feeling of accomplishment that you've experienced
- The things you still want to accomplish, no matter how seemingly far-fetched
- Your career "exit strategy"
- What you hope to gain from this career path over the years to come

In your need to pay the bills, put the kids through college, pay off student loans, and get enough sleep, the 10,000-foot view may be more than you're willing to take on right now, and that's fine. However, bear in mind that it's always there waiting for you, even if you ignore it. The bigger perspective can't be dismissed forever, even if you keep your head under the covers. It's available to you whenever you may need it.

So, Where's Your Devil?

I'm sure you've heard the saying, "the devil's in the details." Well, if you consider the details mentioned above and the 10,000-foot view, where's your devil located? Are you overwhelmed by the day-to-day minutiae, preferring to daydream about the future? Or does the big picture scare you to death as you hide your head in the sand?

Some people's devil may definitely be in the details, but others may actually find comfort in the task-based nature of those details. And since we're nurses, tasks and to-do lists can be our *modus operandi*. But details can actually be a way for us to avoid the big picture.

On the other hand, the person who's "big-picture friendly" may be happy to daydream about the future, making vague plans that won't come to fruition because he or she is unwilling to dig into the details, those things that need to happen on the ground in order for the potential plan to move forward. For such people the devil is certainly in the details, and they will stay in daydream mode for as long as possible so that the details remain comfortably amorphous.

Don't Avoid the Big Picture

If you're a detail person, the big picture may be easy for you to avoid. Those details can keep you busy with your nose to the grindstone, and that tends to keep the big picture at bay.

However, when we focus only on what's at hand, we may lose sight of opportunities that might make themselves known if we were a little more open to the insights and intuitions that the 10,000-foot view provides us.

Sure, the details are important, but if we continue to slog away at something we don't like to do—either out of habit, comfort, or a combination of the two—we may very well be keeping ourselves stuck in a career that's frozen in place, preventing ourselves from moving on to a fulfilling professional identity or role.

The 10,000-foot view can certainly give you vertigo. If you let your creative mind wander freely, it may deliver some ideas that are pretty scary. Your creative professional mind may come up with an entirely new career path, a need or desire to return to school, a brilliant business idea, or something entirely novel and altogether frightening. When you set your mind loose, there's no telling what can happen.

Then again, if you stay in your small, cozy nursing corner without revisiting your dreams and aspirations on occasion, they may remain dormant, and you may slide into professional boredom, lassitude, and maybe even burnout.

Free Your Mind

If I hadn't freed my mind, I would never have taken a chance and begun writing my blog in 2005. Without my creative side waking up, I wouldn't be a freelance nurse writer, a professional nurse podcaster, a Board Certified Nurse Coach, or a public speaker at nursing conferences. Sure, I may have been happy staying in my small nursing corner, but as I listened to the small voice inside of me, that voice clamored more and more loudly for a wider scope of action and exploration.

Not everyone wants to be a coach, writer, podcaster, or blogger, but many of us have aspirations to move beyond where we are. And to "see the forest for the trees," we need to climb to the top of the tallest tree and take a look around.

So, nurses, free your mind, allow yourself to consider the 10,000-foot view, and enjoy the potential expansiveness that you experience, even if you have to tolerate some career vertigo along the way.

CHAPTER 5

Finding the Center of Your Nursing Career

IN SOME SPIRITUAL TRADITIONS there is a notion of finding one's center, the point upon which your life can balance. In your nursing career, finding your center is an important practice, even as you and your life change with time. The center of your career may very well be a moving target. Are you currently in touch with yours?

A Moving Target

The center of your nursing career—the place where you find your deepest satisfaction and soul work—is indeed a moving target. When you first graduate from nursing school, your satisfaction may come from performing your first catheterization or central line dressing change. The novice nurse derives great satisfaction from mastering skills and knowledge, and that is as it should be.

As you move deeper into your career, skills-based learning may feel less satisfying in some ways, depending on your area of practice and specialization. If you approach your clinical work with sincere curiosity and interest, amassing new skills and knowledge may be enough for you, and there may also be times when some new types of experience are called for in order to hold your interest.

Being a staff nurse may work for a while, but you may feel the need to serve as charge nurse, or move into management, administration, research, education, or entrepreneurship. If your body begins to suffer from the rigors of floor nursing, a desk job may seem very attractive.

The moving target of your career and professional and personal happiness is such as it is by necessity. Careers do not naturally stagnate, although some of us fall into professional stagnation by dint of boredom, intellectual laziness, or simply an attachment to what's most comfortable coupled with reasonable or unreasonable fear of the unknown.

Zeroing In

Zeroing in on what makes you tick is an important and ongoing process. In the first years of your nursing career, certain types of experiences will make you happy and keep you fulfilled. As both your professional and personal lives morph over time, your needs as a healthcare professional will also change.

If you get married, have children, suffer personal loss, or live with physical, psychiatric, emotional, or spiritual challenges, your needs vis-à-vis your career will change. As a nursing mother you may choose to work one weekend a month while you raise your children. If your parent is in hospice, you may need to alter your workstyle to fit your lifestyle. And if you go back to school or otherwise change your life, work must adapt apace.

You must always be assessing how you are (or are not) zeroing in on what you want and what will make you happy, both personally and professionally. Perhaps in the last year, simply showing up for your shifts and not harming any patients in the course of your work might have seemed like enough. However, at this time you may feel the need for new challenges, opportunities for growth, and the means to develop as a person.

Zeroing in is not a one-time event; it's a lifelong process.

Your Center

You find your center as a nurse and as a human being by understanding yourself, your dreams, your motivations, your fears, and your desires. What makes you tick? What makes life and work meaningful? What gets you out of bed every morning, and what gets you through the day?

Your emotional and spiritual center at 22 years of age will likely be wildly different than when you're 52, and that 52-year-old self will naturally have different needs than your 82-year-old self. Maslow's hierarchy of needs is a psychological model that consistently holds water. Understand where you are on that hierarchy and feed the part of yourself that's hungry.

Find the center of your life and you'll likely find the center of your career. Find the center of your desires and motivations, and you'll make choices that are meaningful and life-enhancing. Understand the needs that are making themselves known in your heart, mind, and soul, and you'll have a notion of what to do and where to go next. Rather than make choices based on what others are telling you is best, make them based on what you need for your personal and professional development.

Find your center today, tomorrow, next month, and in ten years. It's a moving target, and it's always worth it to keep focused on the bull's-eye.

CHAPTER 6

The Nurse's Magic Wand

OFTEN ASK my coaching clients to verbalize what's next for them in their lives and careers. Based on my contention that nursing and the healthcare industry are their professional oyster, I ask them, "How will you find your pearls?"

Taking this line of thought further, I ask, "What would you do if you had a magic wand, and you could create whatever nursing career you could imagine? What would it look like? Don't worry about how you would do it; this is solely about dreaming big. What's your pleasure?"

A Bold Vision of a Nursing Career

With no holds barred, what is your vision of the ultimate nursing career for you at this point in your life, and perhaps for, let's say, the next decade? What would it be like? What would you like to see and experience?

If you'd like to indulge me, the following exercise may help you create a vision of what you want in your career.

Close your eyes, and sink into a few nice, deep abdominal breaths. Remind yourself that this is not a time for your logical mind to find reasons that you'll never have what you're able to visualize. *To the contrary,* this is a time to think big, with no self-imposed limitations, and no concerns for what's possible or "impossible."

Now, when you're fully relaxed and have taken those deep breaths, continue to breathe in a way that will allow you to stay in that calm, centered place.

Picture your ultimate work environment. Walk through the front door. What does it look like? What colors are painted on the walls? What does it smell like? Is there light streaming through the windows? Are there plants in optimal locations, and attractive art adorning the rooms? Do you have an office or desk? What is your personal work environment like?

What area of nursing are you practicing and loving? When you picture your optimal colleagues, what are they like, and how do they treat one another? What sort of atmosphere exists between you and your coworkers? Is there collaboration and openness? Are people transparent and supportive? Does administration give the support that's needed and desired?

Taking this further, how much are you paid for your work? What's your schedule like? How's your commute? How do you feel when you get home after a day's work? Do you look forward to returning the next day?

Your ideal workplace may feel like a dream, but it's a dream that can be sought after and manifested in your life to some degree, especially if you're thoughtful and careful about what you really want, and take inspired action to find or create it.

Manifesting Your Ideal

While it might sound like a New Age daydream to visualize your ideal job, isn't it better than continuing to complain about what you don't have, and how you'll never find anything better? If you can picture in your mind what you'd truly like to experience, don't you think it's much more likely that—just maybe—you'll put more energy into finding or creating work that might fulfill at least some of your criteria?

Let's face it, if you spend every day saying to yourself, "This job is horrible, and I'll never find another job that's any better anyway, so I may as well just suck it up," do you think you'll be motivated to keep looking, networking, and trying to up your game and move on to a better situation? A defeatist, negative attitude will likely net you a career that matches that attitude pretty exactly, so why not spend time picturing what you want rather than what you don't want, or what you believe you can't have or perhaps feel you don't really deserve?

Sure, health care can be a tough industry, and nursing can be a challenging profession with many negative aspects that are hard to swallow. That said, since I assume you have to work no matter what, why not continue to focus on what you want while also advocating for change in your present situation? Why not spend your energy on visualizing the kind of work environment, career, and colleagues that would make your professional life more of a pleasant adventure and less of a rat race?

It's Always Possible to Find the Pearls

If your eyes are on the prize—even a prize beyond your current situation—perhaps that prize will come that much closer to reality every day you focus on the ultimate scenario that will make your nurse's heart sing.

Anything is possible, and everyone has some pearls out there in the deep, blue nursing ocean. It's up to you to find where yours are hiding, and if you can't find them, build your own from scratch.

Positive, supportive, and wonderful work environments for nurses do exist, especially when thoughtful people like us demand them and create them.

Now, wave your magic wand and get to work creating what you want!

CHAPTER 7

The Polymath Nurse

NURSES NEED TO KNOW a lot of things; nursing professionals have knowledge of anatomy, physiology, pathophysiology, human behavior, human growth and development, the nursing process, research, biostatistics, and many more subjects than you can shake a syringe at. Nurses' knowledge is vast; we are all potentially nurse polymaths.

What Is a Polymath?

Wikipedia defines *polymath* as "a person whose expertise spans a significant number of different subject areas; such a person is known to draw on complex bodies of knowledge to solve specific problems." Merriam-Webster dictionary states that a polymath is "someone who knows a lot about many different things."

My go-to example of a polymath is none other than Leonardo da Vinci. He was a painter, inventor, scientist, mathematician, engineer, writer, and even a paleontologist.

27

Leonardo went way beyond being a cool Ninja Turtle; he was a symbol of what is sometimes referred to as a "Renaissance Man," which I would now call a "Renaissance Person."

Polymaths often move culture and society forward in ways we can't even measure due to the far-reaching depth and breadth of their influence. So, you may ask, what do polymaths have to do with nursing? Please indulge me, dear reader.

The Nurse As Polymath

Let's say you work in a busy ICU, CCU, or med-surg unit. The patients you care for are medically complex, and when you pull the camera back and examine their lives from a holistic viewpoint, you can see that their circumstances beyond the hospital bed are incredibly multifaceted and complex.

For patients with addiction, mental illness, and multiple comorbidities, providing care can be a tricky business that calls for great tact, sensitivity, compassion, and an understanding of the challenges faced by the patient and his or her family. Socioeconomics, education, and many other factors collide to complicate medical care, and the astute nurse may need to address more than just meds, IV pumps, and symptom management.

In home health, my area of nursing specialty, nurses must sometimes act as family counselors, plumbers, and carpenters, not to mention clinicians. Nurse entrepreneurs are also polymath material, sometimes straddling the worlds of business and clinical nursing on a daily basis. So, many nurses are probably polymaths and don't even know it.

Making a Case for the Nurse Polymath

Why would a nurse want to consciously choose to stoke the fires of polymathism in his or her life? What benefit would a nurse derive from actually making this a goal?

A nurse clinician polymath is a multifaceted health professional who approaches patient care and the nursing process with eyes wide open and curiosity on high alert. Nurse polymaths read voraciously, but not just about nursey stuff; they read about culture, society, politics, art, economics, or anything else that deserves attention. Their breadth of knowledge can be applied to solving problems in sophisticated and creative ways.

In business, the nurse entrepreneur polymath may take a deep dive into social media, become an expert in WordPress, learn to use accounting software, study emotional intelligence, create an app, and write a series of books. The polymath business owner isn't necessarily a master of everything or a novice at most things. The polymath knows enough to be proficient or conversant with what's necessary, with natural curiosity being a driving force behind continued learning and increased mastery.

Nurse polymaths understand the currents moving through culture and society, absorbing what informs and strengthens their work in the world.

The Polymath Curse?

"Jack (or Jill) of all trades and master of none" is a saying that many of us grew up hearing. In a complex 21st-century world, becoming a polymath can seem like a form of intellectual attention deficit self-torture. We can certainly fall into a trap of trying to know it all and ultimately knowing too little about a lot to make a difference. No one can possibly consume all the information that's out there.

Leonardo obviously didn't know everything. Granted, he lived in a much less complex time, but there were certainly areas of life and living that his intellect didn't aspire to conquer. Like Leonardo, we need to discriminate and not try to master too many subjects. And there's another drawback to consider. Some of us have probably known people who worked hard to be well-read and erudite, but who perhaps seemed so engrossed in their minds that they couldn't relate to people.

Intellectualism for its own sake isn't the goal; rather, finding the areas we're drawn to and honing in on our true passions can help us to become polymaths who are well-rounded yet measured in the breadth of what we strive to tackle.

Polymathism doesn't have to be all about book learning, either. A polymath may be highly emotionally intelligent, insightful, with a sincere and deep grasp of human nature and suffering.

The Balanced Nurse Polymath

The balanced nurse polymath has areas of expertise that he or she delves into with gusto, creativity, and enthusiasm.

My areas of professional expertise include writing, podcasting, social media, and coaching, and I have a few other areas that are also relatively strong. However, when it comes to accounting, complex tech issues, coding, or building websites, I have others do those tasks for me because they simply don't interest me enough to make time to learn—or I'm just too plain busy to bother. When I was a homeowner, I hired out for everything because my skills as a handyman are pretty abysmal. This polymath doesn't do plumbing and carpentry. Or windows.

Otherwise, I have a fairly solid store of knowledge related to certain types of music, art, and literature, and there are some other subjects that similarly draw me in. I don't try to know it all, but my interests are broad enough to keep me on my toes and constantly learning, reading, and growing in my areas of greatest interest.

Balanced polymathism can truly serve the nurse who wishes to be well-rounded. You can't know everything about everything, but you can know a significant amount about the many things that speak to you most deeply. At the very least it can lead to interests outside of nursing that can create greater balance and happiness in your life.

Polymath nurses, it's time to come out of the closet; spread your polymath wings, read your books, expand your knowledge, learn that which makes you happy, and use that knowledge and understanding to be a better person, a more skilled clinician, a more informed citizen, and a more powerful and effective nurse.

CHAPTER 8

The Nursing Class Hero

FANS OF JOHN LENNON might bristle at my adulteration of the title of a famous song by the iconic musician and peace activist, but a "nursing class hero" is certainly something to be.

Listening to Lennon's "Working Class Hero," I realized that, aside from being a great play on words, "nursing class hero" could also be a fitting and interesting way to explore our profession from a novel perspective.

Nursing and Class

Back in the day, nursing was a nonprofessional, relatively unskilled form of labor where nurses were at the beck and call of all-powerful physicians.

For a long time the nursing profession lacked any quantifiable scientific data or practices that verifiably documented our contributions, thus we were relegated to a working class existence without significant recognition, remuneration, or respect (the "Three R's" I focus on in chapter 16).

Despite the fact that Florence Nightingale is credited by many scholars with essentially inventing the notion of public health (even though she reportedly did not readily embrace the germ theory), nursing remained in the background of health care for decades.

During the 20th century, nursing was often considered a "pink collar" job, meaning it was generally a profession pursued mostly by women (and men who couldn't manage to become doctors because they were too poor, too weak, or otherwise unmotivated by power, money, and status). Teachers were generally labeled "pink collar," as well as food service workers, maids, childcare providers, secretaries, flight attendants, and others. You get the picture.

Thus, the "profession" of nursing was diminished in the eyes of the patriarchal power brokers as a woman's vocation with limited prestige and importance.

So, what changed?

Nursing Claims Its Place

I'm certainly no scholar of the history of nursing, but I surmise that the late 20th century and early 21st century saw clear demonstrations that nursing belongs in the ranks of professions that are seen as crucial and deserving of increased pay, status, and recognition.

Perhaps it was the rise of nursing scholarship and research that paved the way. Perhaps it was the notion that nursing is actually based on a scientific body of knowledge wholly separate from but related to medical knowledge. Perhaps it was because nurses began to value themselves and demand respect and recognition for their individual and collective contribution to the health and well-being of the nation and the world.

Moreover, maybe it was the fact that nurses had moved beyond hospital-based diploma programs, wholeheartedly embracing academia and earning associate degrees, baccalaureate degrees, and even master's and doctoral degrees. And perhaps it was just a combination—a "perfect storm"—of factors that tipped the scales in our favor.

We Are Trusted

As I love to mention over and over again (am I gloating?), nurses continue to claim the status of being the most trusted professionals in the United States. At any party or gathering, say you're a nurse and you automatically gain the trust and gratitude of many people who express their love of nurses, followed by the occasional story of a "nurse angel" who lives in their memory.

As a nurse, you also gain the distinction of being the go-to person in your neighborhood or family for advice, questions, and medical counsel, for better or worse.

Despite the popular characters of Nurse Ratched, Nurse Jackie, and others who taint the profession in various ways, the general public still holds us in overall high esteem, and declaring your "nurseness" has many benefits (but apparently no regular discounts at the movies, the airline ticket counter, or other places where it counts).

Let's Ditch the Collar, Shall We?

Blue collar, white collar, pink collar, green collar, ring around the collar—what does it all mean, anyway? Is it even relevant anymore? These artificial designations are a way for those in positions of power to categorize us for their own ends. We don't have to accept their categories any more than we need to accept their erroneous and misguided beliefs in their own significance.

Nurses have power. Nurses are powerful. Nurses wield knowledge, compassion, skill, insight, and the depth and breadth of their experience.

As the population ages and nurses become even more indispensable in the promotion of healthy lifestyles and preventive wellness practices, our ability to impact the health of the nation and world will increase exponentially.

As doctors continue to leave primary care in pursuit of the salaries and status of specialization, it is nurses (many prepared with master's and doctoral degrees) who continue to fill the gap by caring for those in need of solid, scientific, and compassionate primary care. Nurse practitioners are seeing expanding autonomy and significant projected job growth, and that is a testament to their importance. Nursing's day has come.

Seize the Day

I don't think John Lennon would mind my borrowing his song title (and the spirit of that powerful ditty) for a play on words that underscores the importance and power of nurses. In fact, I bet he'd proudly walk in picket lines with union nurses demanding equal pay, improved working conditions, and safer patient care.

Yes, I can indeed say that a "nursing class hero" is something to be.

CHAPTER 9

Your Nursing Career and a Latte

DRINKING A LATTE (decaf—I'm an unapologetic caffeine lightweight) makes me realize there's a very appropriate metaphor related to nurses, nursing, and a perfectly brewed latte. It may sound silly, but it may be more apt than you imagine.

So, think about a latte for a moment. Its base is espresso, a rich, dense shot of coffee awesomeness that boasts deep flavor and a cultural history worthy of movies, books, and a great number of rabid fans around the world. Poured into and over that (hopefully) perfect shot or two of espresso is a quantity of expertly steamed milk. And when it's done right, the result is nothing short of miraculous in its creaminess, artfulness, and foamy aesthetic pleasure.

Lattes with a delicate hat of foam can be decorated by talented baristas who take the time to apply their expertise in order to create a visual and culinary experience that delights the senses of appreciative coffee drinkers. Is your mouth watering yet? Craving a cup? I think I am!

The Espresso of Your Nurseness

As your nursing career is imbued with depth and breadth of experience, knowledge, skill, and nurse wisdom, your nurseness is like an espresso bean that has reached its peak of flavor and robustness. Your nurseness grows over time, and it takes on flavor and characteristics from everything it comes into contact with.

A coffee bean is kissed by sun, watered by rain, fed by soil, exposed to the air, and then roasted to perfection. Similarly, your skills and knowledge as a nurse are also fed, watered, coddled, and roasted in the fires of the nursing profession (pardon the mash-up of metaphors).

Where is your nurseness in terms of its development of a ripe and robust flavor? Is your career still young, enjoying the fertility of learning and soaking up the nutrients of experience? Or is your career fully ripe and bursting with the flavors of all you've seen and done?

As a mature nursing professional with significant experience under your belt, you're like a perfect espresso: satisfying, flavorful, robust, and earthy. As a newer nurse, you're already developing the flavor and depth of your chosen career.

Don't Forget the Foam

The steamed milk and foam that are poured into and over the espresso of your nursing career and nurseness are like the cherry on top of a sundae. The foam may be represented by a special certification or training, deep self-knowledge and self-awareness, keen emotional intelligence, additional degrees and academic achievements, or a vertical move into management or executive nursing leadership.

The foam you add to the recipe of your nursing career is a rich froth whipped up from all you've accomplished and achieved.

The Tools of the Trade

A plain old resume created without much creativity or thoughtfulness is more like a cup of coffee brewed in a diner than a latte made by an artful barista. When you're putting together or editing your resume, does it come across as bland and generic or heartfully prepared for maximum impact? How can you make it more like a beautiful latte, with depth of flavor showcasing the measure of your nursing career, as well as a foamy topping that demonstrates a regard for beauty and aesthetics?

Cover letters can also be small works of letter-writing art, with flawless construction and a personalized, nongeneric flavor. On the other hand, cover letters can sometimes seem like instant coffee, something made without much thought or care.

Adding Spice to Your Career

Just as we add cinnamon, cocoa powder, nutmeg, or flavored syrups to our lattes and coffee drinks, we can also add spice to our careers. A stint with Doctors Without Borders gives you a certain leg up on other candidates, as does having Johns

Hopkins on your resume. You can also spice up your nursing resume and career with various forms of volunteerism, leadership roles, research activities, or awards demonstrating your commitment to excellence.

Building a robust professional network also adds to the spice of your career. Your contacts and valued colleagues are those who will write amazing letters of recommendation, endorse you on LinkedIn, serve as excellent references, and otherwise support your professional journey. They're like sprinkles of dark chocolate shavings on the latte of your nursing career.

Be Flavorful, Nurses

In order to stand out in the job marketplace, you need to be flavorful and unique. If you're as generic as diner coffee, you won't necessarily be as attractive to potential employers as you would if you were unique, flavorful, and thoughtfully presented.

Is your career a latte, a cappuccino, or a perfect Americano or cold brew? Consider the flavor you want your nursing career to have. Bring those flavors forward with conscious effort and thoughtful consideration of how you can take your career to the next level, whether it's decaffeinated, half-caff, or high test. Happy brewing!

CHAPTER 10

Playing Big in Your Nursing Career

HAVE YOU EVER PLAYED SMALL in your life or nursing career? Have you taken the path of least resistance or otherwise ignored the inner voice that's pushing you to greater heights or bigger risks—as a nurse or as a human being? Have you played small when you really wanted to play big? You're not alone!

We've all played it small at certain times in our lives, even when we knew we needed to think bigger. There are plenty of voices inside of us (and outside of us!) that compel us to not take risks, to do what others say we should, and to ignore our inner yearnings and intuition.

Nurses hear a lot of "shoulds" throughout their careers, beginning in nursing school, and continuing until (and after) retirement:

- You should be a doctor, not a nurse.
- You should get a job in med-surg.

- You shouldn't get a job in med-surg.
- School nursing isn't really nursing.
- You can't start a business; nurses aren't business owners.
- You should go to grad school.
- You shouldn't go to grad school.
- There are no nursing jobs
- You shouldn't quit.
- You should _____.
- You shouldn't _____.

If I had listened to the naysayers, I wouldn't have pursued my passion and followed my gut by beginning a long and fruitful career in ambulatory care, community nursing, home care, hospice, and public health. They all said I should get a job in med-surg, but my gut said otherwise. I followed my gut, and I never looked back.

If I'd believed the notion that nurses can't be business owners or entrepreneurs, I never would have taken the risk of writing, blogging, podcasting, becoming a career coach, or doing all the amazing things I now have the privilege of doing in my career.

What have you chosen not to do because others were "shoulding" on you? Where have you played it small when you wanted to play it big? What choices have you made where you wanted to do more and you chose to do less because "they" said it was safer that way? When did you want to be risky and you instead chose to be safe?

Nurses, you don't have to play it safe. Life isn't always about risk aversion and the avoidance of uncertainty, pain, suffering, or the great unknown.

They can "should" you to death, but you can also close your ears to what they say you need to do. You can ignore the safe advice; you can choose the less familiar path.

Now, no one said it would be easy to go against the grain, and there's always a risk that you'll fall on your face. But you know what? You took a risk by coming through that birth canal and taking your first breath. You took a risk by becoming a nurse and putting yourself on the line to care for others in times of great vulnerability. You took a risk by reading this chapter about playing it big.

I'm not going to tell you that you have to play it big; you can play small any time you choose. I'm also not going to say that you're "less than" if you choose a safe, well-worn path as a nurse or as a human being. And remember, one person's small may be another person's big – it's all relative.

The main message here is that you get to choose your own path, ignoring those who project their fear onto you in a conscious or unconscious effort to hold you back.

Nurses, if you want to risk it, go for it. If you want to play it safe, please do. Choose your own adventure. Play the game by your own darn rules, whether those rules call for incredible risk or simple, safe adherence to a sure-fire path.

Florence Nightingale didn't play it safe by going to the Crimea and single-handedly creating the practice of applied biostatistics while transforming the care of injured soldiers for centuries to come. No, good old Florence disregarded Victorian convention, flouted her parents' plans for a domestic life of 19th-century safety, and created a legacy that reverberates to this day.

You don't have to be the next Florence Nightingale or Jean Watson; you just have to be the next iteration of whoever you want to be.

Dream it. Risk it. Choose it. Be it.

CHAPTER 11

Building Your Nursing Career House

A S A NURSE, the house of your nursing career must stand on a solid foundation. Once that foundation has been laid, your career can be built in the form of any structure you see fit. How are you building the house of your nursing career?

Start With a Foundation

Every career must be built on a foundation of skill, knowledge, and expertise. Formal education is one way we begin to build that foundation, although in previous generations apprenticeship was the vehicle of acquiring what was needed to succeed in a particular trade.

As a nurse, your foundation is built by cinder blocks of expertise acquired during your nursing school experiences, and as a novice nurse, you continue to hone skills that need more practice, and you acquire new knowledge along the way. If you begin to specialize in a specific form of nursing, the particular knowledge base of that area of focus becomes central to the architecture of your career.

An Artist's Touch

In every nursing professional's career there are moments when the nurse must make a determination if he or she is going to take the tried and true path, the well-worn track, or deviate from the norm and build a career house that's a bit different, a little out of the ordinary.

You can bring an artist's touch to the way you build your nursing career. Frank Lloyd Wright designed homes, office buildings, and museums that completely subverted architectural norms. He was unapologetic in his rejection of the status quo, and he forged ahead with dogged persistence. His path was not easy, but it was, in the end, his and his alone.

Your nursing career house does not need to look like anyone else's; it doesn't have to resemble the careers you were told were exemplars of what a "normal" nurse follows. Some architects stick with modes of building that everyone expects, and the results can indeed be perfectly suitable. However, the tried and true path can sometimes feel stale or unoriginal, and taking a meandering journey may be what works for some who choose to differentiate from the norm.

Just as a woodworker may make the interior of a home unique and idiosyncratic, your nursing career can also be a work of art created from your imagination. Remember, the foundation holds it all together, but your embellishments will make it your own, not to mention the radical styles of success you create with your mind, heart, and soul.

Embellish As You Wish

In the 21st century, there are nurse writers, nurse filmmakers, nurse podcasters, and nurse artists. Some nurses are creating new types of businesses and positions that are devoid of any clinical identity whatsoever, but they still consider themselves nurses.

There are several members of Congress who are nurses, and while a Congressperson may not have time to work as a nurse, their "nurseness" may, or perhaps must, to some extent inform who they are, how they think, and what they do.

Your career house may have a tin roof, a slate roof, or a roof made of high-tech mini solar panels. You may choose to heat the house of your career with the fuel of creative pursuits (art, music, filmmaking, podcasting) or with the fuel of intellectual prowess (a PhD, an added degree in law, or perhaps the writing of books that inspire the next generation of nurses to even greater heights).

Creation, Destruction, and Everything Between

Whether you build a career house of brick, straw, adobe, or Grecian columns is up to you. Once the foundation is laid, your house can be whatever you desire. Moreover, if your house gets old, if the walls crack, or the paint begins to peel, you can always give it a fresh coat of paint, do some demolition, add an extra room, or build a new wing.

If your nursing career house feels claustrophobic and limited, you can put in a window for a breath of fresh air. A window in your career's house may look out upon a vista you haven't considered before, like writing, teaching, leaving the hospital environment, or starting a business. Tearing down a wall or doing some demolition may be necessary when what you've been doing has come to a natural end, and you must take down the walls of limitation so you can see what's next and build something new.

Your nursing career house may have scaffolding when under construction, and it may sometimes feel drafty as you build a fresh new structure to live in as a nurse. The wiring and plumbing may feel dodgy when you're uncertain about what's next, and you may have to flush a lot of waste down the toilet if your self-worth has taken some hits over the years and you need to expel outmoded ways of thinking.

Cut the Ribbon

When you've come through a period of career demolition and reconstruction, the dust will eventually settle. As that dust clears, you can get out a broom and dustpan, mop the floor, paint the walls, and then invite everyone to the ceremony when you're ready to cut the ribbon on the new iteration of the house of your nursing career. Whether you're launching a new business or simply changing specialties, invite others to share in your excitement and joy.

Whenever your nursing career transitions to its next iteration, stand back, admire your handiwork, and dance into your new career home, built from the sweat equity of your own labor, thought, ambition, and love. Celebrate!

CHAPTER 12

Half Full or Half Empty?

I'T'S NO SECRET that there's a multitude of unhappy nurses out there in the world. From mandatory overtime to unhealthy nurse-patient ratios, I admit there are very valid reasons for this seeming epidemic of discontent. So, is the nursing glass half full or half empty? I guess it depends on who you're drinking with (and perhaps what you're drinking).

Reasons to Be Cheerful—Or Not

This chapter isn't really about the multitude of reasons that explain nurses' rampant unhappiness. A new study mentioned recently on Twitter states that a full one-third of nurses are unhappy with either their jobs or their careers. I get it.

There are also nurses who say, "I love my work, but I hate my job." I get that too.

Sadly, it's a given that too many nurses work in environments that are unhealthy, unsupportive, demanding, and backbreaking, and that's indeed a sad state of affairs.

It's Who You Talk To

Taking into consideration the relative level of discontent in the nursing profession, your worldview can be significantly influenced by who you talk to and who you spend time with. The tenor of the conversation among your nursing colleagues will, of course, influence your perspective, so think about who your conversational partners are—and who they could be.

If your Thursday morning coffee klatsch is regularly attended by jaded nurses who spend the hour railing against the hospital and gossiping about doctors and interns (and one another), there's a definite downside to the time you spend at that particular table.

And if your idea of a good time is focusing on what's wrong, then there are plenty of nurses who'll eagerly buy you another round in order to keep you waxing negative, thus justifying and solidifying their own negative bias.

"Bartender, another round of 'Negatinis,' please."

Let's Be Realistic

Like I said toward the beginning of this chapter, I get it. There's a lot that's wrong with the picture in both nursing and the wider world of health care. That's a given. At the same time, there are nurses, doctors, administrators, and theorists who really want to make it right. Fighting the good fight to make things better is a noble cause, and many are called to engage in that particular battle. Kudos to them.

Other nurses, tired of the mainstream game, have dipped their toes into entrepreneurship, and dived into satisfying careers that defy the very notion of what it even means to be a nurse. Kudos to them, too.

And some are creating new opportunities for themselves within the mainstream healthcare system, leveraging their skills as coaches, consultants, IT gurus, and all manner of novel yet robust professional roles. Kudos all around.

There's a place for everyone at the table. In fact, you can even build your own table if the current ones don't quite match your vision of what your career could be.

Nurse's Choice

So, you can talk to the jaded, cynical, and burned-out nurses who just want to see the glass as perpetually half empty, or you can interact with the nurses who are the positive role models and forward thinkers of the profession who definitely view the glass as perpetually half full.

It's tiring to hang out with the jaded and cynical complainers, but it can be energizing (and fun!) to hang out with the optimistic nurses who are actively making their careers the best they can be.

Who are you talking to and spending time with? Are you drinking the bitter and cynical dregs of nursing station coffee? Are you pounding down "Negatinis" with unhappy abandon? Or are you drinking from the cup of optimism, sharing with your colleagues a vision of what's possible, even as you acknowledge the stark realities of 21st-century health care?

The choice is yours, my friends, and I invite you to my table, where we serve Positive Punch and Optimism Smoothies.

Thirsty?

CHAPTER 13

Feeding Your Nursing Career

Y OUR NURSING CAREER is a lot like your body; it needs to be fed, watered, exercised, and well-rested in order to function optimally. How do you choose to optimize the nutrition you feed to your body every day? Are you conscientious about eating enough fruits and vegetables? Do you monitor your intake of saturated fat? Are you drinking enough water and exercising? Do you avoid processed foods and soda? As you care for your body, you should also be caring for your nursing career.

What kinds of nutrition does your career need? What nutritional deficits does your nursing career demonstrate? Are you willing to feed your career as well as you feed your own body?

Individualized Career Nutrition

Optimal nutrition for your nursing career may be quite dissimilar from that of your friends or colleagues. One nurse's career might thrive on continuing education, attending clinical conferences, and learning new bedside nursing skills.

For another nurse, her career nutrition means claiming her place as a dancer, learning to integrate her love of dance with her love of being a caregiver, perhaps through offering movement classes for nurses in need of self-care.

Your nursing career nutrition may be spiritual, emotional, intellectual, psychological, or none of the above. While we may sometimes want a prescription for what we need to do on our professional journey (e.g., get a job in med-surg, earn an MSN, get a doctorate, work in the ICU), not every nurse is going to travel the same path as her nurse brothers and sisters. This can seem like both a blessing and a curse.

Nutrition Changes With Time

Would you eat the same way when you're 55 as when you were 25? Probably not; in fact, I hope not. Our nutritional needs change over time, and those of us who are paying attention know when to change gears as we age. Let's face it, we can't overindulge in our 50s like we did in our teens; our bodies just can't take the punishment we inflicted on them back in the day.

So, if you need to alter your nutrition as you age and change, doesn't it follow that you would also need to alter your career's nutrition in the same manner?

When you're fresh out of nursing school, you're like a sponge; there's so much you haven't yet experienced. Every catheterization, blood draw, and central line dressing change has the potential to be a revelation. After 20 years or so, perhaps there's less novelty, and the new clinical skills you can pick up along the way just don't bring the same level of excitement and accomplishment.

If you feel tapped out and your nursing career is feeling a little anemic or dehydrated, it may be time to inject something new into your career diet. In other words, get something new on your plate. Whether it's a class related directly to nursing, or a program that teaches you how to launch a podcast, something novel can break the spell of your career ennui and open your eyes to something new and exciting.

When we get bored with a cookbook we've used for ten years, do we just keep cooking the same old recipes over and over again? No, we don't. If we need a cookbook to make anything more than cereal and coffee, we'll likely go out and get ourselves another one and deliberately bring some novelty into the kitchen.

Your career's nutritional needs will change, just like your body will crave different types of foods at different stages of development. Pay attention to what you're feeding your nursing career.

A Nutritional Assessment

Here's my prescription for a nutritional assessment of your career. Ask yourself the following questions:

- How do I feed my nursing career?
- What is my career asking of me?

- Am I satisfied with how my nursing career is in this very moment?
- What am I craving as a nurse?
- What experiences/knowledge/skills would be fulfilling and enlivening?
- What would I like my nursing career to look like in 5 years? 10 years? 20 years?
- How can I optimize my career's nutritional intake?

A nutritional assessment of your nursing career means looking honestly and nakedly at what makes you tick as a nurse. If you've been hiding from your own feelings about your career as you silently burn out, this process could be somewhat painful. Those who have been avoiding their feelings about their lives as nurses may need to wash their face with cold water and brace for a dose of reality.

Doing such an assessment of your nursing career may arrive at the choice to leave your clinical position and open a consulting practice, free from the bedside and nursing documentation. This assessment process could lead to a decision to (gulp!) go back to school and earn your PhD because, for better or worse, your professional goals simply aren't going to come to fruition without those three letters after your name.

Feed Your Career What It Wants

Asking yourself these types of questions means being willing to listen to the answers and then feed your career what it's asking for. If your body was dehydrated, would you deny it sodium and water? If you had scurvy, would you choose not to eat foods rich in vitamin C? If you had diabetes, would you just shovel donuts into your mouth every day? If your career is calling for a certain diet, it's your duty and responsibility to give it what it needs to thrive.

Burnout and compassion fatigue don't just happen in a vacuum. If you can keep your career nutrition healthy, consume the right professional diet, and immerse yourself in a professional environment that truly feeds your soul, you're on the path to a healthy, well-fed, and satisfying nursing career.

CHAPTER 14

A Shot of Nursing Self-Esteem

DO YOU HOLD YOURSELF and your nursing skills in high esteem? Do you internalize and embody your value as a nurse? If not, it's high time you did.

Most of us have voices in our heads that attempt to derail our self-esteem or throw us off our game. Those voices may harken back to a parent, grandparent, teacher, or other individual who devalued us or threw a wrench into our self-worth.

There are plenty of signs that nurses are valued by society, the Gallup poll being one such measure of how the public trusts and honors us. However, nurses are also demeaned in media, treated as sex objects, and frequently portrayed as simple handmaidens to doctors, lacking any scientific or clinical knowledge and expertise of their own.

In speaking with my career-coaching clients who are nurses, I often detect hints of low self-esteem, shadows that diminish their ability or willingness to believe in themselves. Nurses say things like:

- *"I don't really matter in the scheme of things."*
- *"The doctor doesn't respect me."*
- *"My opinion doesn't seem to count."*
- *"I feel like an impostor."*

Do you say or think things like this? Do you feel "less than" in your work as a nurse? Are there voices that keep you down and make you feel diminished?

What Types of Knowledge Do You Carry?

As nurses, we carry many types of knowledge. Yes, there's clinical knowledge, and that can certainly mushroom to encyclopedic proportions over time. Clinical knowledge is great, and that's the kind of knowledge we would generally consider when thinking about nurses and nursing.

However, there are many more types of knowledge and personal genius, and these carry just as much value as clinical data or skill, perhaps even more.

Institutional knowledge is priceless. If you are an integral member of a facility, agency, or institution, your knowledge of the underpinnings and machinations of that institution cannot be underestimated in terms of value. Institutional knowledge allows you to navigate the organization, find resources, connect one part of the company to another, and act as a valuable liaison and keeper of the culture.

Emotional knowledge is also crucial. As nurses, we connect with our patients on an emotional-psychic level, perhaps even on a spiritual level at times. You may be an astute clinician, but you may also have a level of emotional intelligence or genius that sets you apart. Your insight and intuition may lead you to deep places with your patients or colleagues, and your value may lie in your ability to see into situations in a way others cannot.

Relational knowledge and practical relational intelligence impact institutional and emotional knowledge directly. If you carry relational genius into your nursing practice, your emotional connections with patients are even more profound due to your ability to take that emotional knowledge and leverage it in your relationships.

Some nurses may be emotionally intuitive but not have the innate or learned skills to communicate those emotions and intuitions to their patients or colleagues. However, if you are also a relational person with powerful networking and people skills, your institutional knowledge will be strengthened by your navigation of relationships, building of bonds, and strong abilities for nurturing bonds and connections over time.

Other types of knowledge may include "hard skills" like computer programming, software design, plumbing, or engineering; training in other disciplines (e.g., massage, Reiki, coaching, business, hospitality, customer service); or other esoteric or nonesoteric fields of knowledge.

Your nursing knowledge goes deep and spans many disciplines, and you bring all of that to the table .

Self-Administer a Vaccine of Value

If your nursing self-esteem needs a booster shot, how can you self-administer that vaccine? First, you can make a list of the various types of knowledge you carry as a nurse, including former careers, subjects you've studied in school, and knowledge and skill you've accumulated by self-study and workshops.

Once you've made that list, consider how those skills impact your nursing care, and how they add value to your patient care, research, teaching, management, supervision of others, or however else you function as a nurse.

If you need support in coming up with concrete examples of your value, ask trusted colleagues, friends, or family members to help you. This can be a booster vaccine, and can be injected whenever you need it most. Have them fill out a questionnaire, or just unabashedly query them about how they see you. You may be surprised just how valued and "seen" you are.

You need to vaccinate yourself against low nursing self-esteem; learning to acknowledge, internalize, and embody your multifaceted value is key.

CHAPTER 15

Direct the Film of Your Nursing Career!

THERE'S SOMETHING TO SAY about being in control, isn't there? And when you think about your nursing career, do you feel like you're in control, or are you allowing yourself to be a bit actor when you should actually be the star? It's up to you to seize the director's chair and begin directing the film of your career. Are you ready?

From the day you enter nursing school until the time you retire from nursing, it can often feel like you're not in control. You're told where to go to clinical, who your patients will or won't be, what classes you should take, what specialty to focus on, what advanced degree to pursue, and whether you can or can't take a lunch break or go to the bathroom during a shift.

At times it may seem like there's a whole lot of acquiescing and control going on in nursing, and even though the movie of your life is all about you, it may feel like someone else is directing the film of your career.

Take the Helm

Taking the helm and directing your own career means you don't go to graduate school just because "they" say you should. Who are "they," anyway? Taking the helm means, even though everyone tells you that you should get two years of med-surg under your belt, you have a different idea of what to do when you get out of nursing school. And you do it.

Taking the helm may mean launching an entrepreneurial venture when everyone says that it's doomed to fail. Daring nurses do daring things and take calculated risks, and in the film of your nursing career your calculated risk may be to hang a shingle and launch a practice as a coach, writer, or consultant.

When you take the helm and assume control, you become not only the director of your film, you begin to write the plot and dialogue, choose the supporting cast, and scout for locations that are the best fit for your vision of the ultimate outcome.

The Supporting Cast

The supporting cast and costars of the film of your nursing career should be kind, good team players, and able to play the part with grace. Your teammates need not be bullies, authoritarian father figures, grouches, complainers, or slackers who let you do all the heavy lifting.

Finding the right cast for your career film may not be easy, but if you happen to locate the supporting players who can really make the film a success, it will feel like you've found your long lost tribe.

You must use discretion, intuition, and your good nursing karma to find the place of your dreams where your colleagues are all that you want them to be. It may never be perfect, but you deserve an environment populated with coworkers—the cast—that will drive you to success and satisfaction, not distress and dissatisfaction.

Scouting a Location

Real estate agents are known to say that it's all about location, location, location. When you interview for a job, you may not know what you're truly getting into until you're actually there, but as you begin working, you'll see signs that let you know whether you've scouted a good venue for filming or not.

A workplace where bullies are tolerated is not a location for you to write the script of your career as a nurse. An environment where people are beaten down, micromanaged, split into warring parties, or otherwise abused is not the place where you want to set up your film crew and make your movie.

Even though you may need to test drive some losers in order to eventually find your ideal workplace, finding a location that supports your creativity and ability as a nurse is like finding gold for your career. Healthy, conscious, and progressive workplaces are out there, folks; you just have to use your nose and find them.

The location where you play out the tragedy and comedy of nursing and healthcare is important. You may spend more time at work than you do at home, so make sure you're in a supportive environment that brings out the best in you. After all, you're the star of the show.

Stay Focused

Just as a camera needs to be focused to capture the action, so do your mind and heart need to remain focused and aware.

No one says nursing is easy, and we all know that some workplaces and colleagues won't lend themselves well to the successful completion of the film of your career. Many factors will work against you: miserable colleagues, poor work environments, and fellow cast members who just don't know their lines and the right way to create a viable and successful portrayal of nursing at its best.

There are things you can control and things you can't. When you're being bullied, you can either work to get rid of the bully, or you can remove yourself from that workplace. If your colleagues are miserable wretches and the work environment is less than friendly, you can try to be a change agent or you can bail. Even big stars will sometimes walk off the set, and sometimes even the crew will go on strike. Don't put up with anything that will make you miserable or sick and tired of nursing.

The film of your nursing career should of course be the story of the trials and tribulations of your life as a nurse, but it should also chronicle your successes, epiphanies, and moments of glory and satisfaction.

Seize the helm of your career film, choose your cast of colleagues well, and scout the location that's best for you.

You hold the camera and you control the film's production. Make it count. Make it work for you. And make it the best movie it can possibly be.

CHAPTER 16

The Three R's of Nursing

THERE ARE SOME very basic things that nurses look for—and deserve—in the course of their nursing careers. It's clear that this list could probably be expanded to include many other ideas as well. I've identified "three R's" of nursing: respect, remuneration, and recognition.

Initially, nursing was an unskilled form of labor, but over time nursing became more skilled and professional. Now more nurses usually receive the recognition, remuneration, and respect they deserve.

Let's examine each one the three R's.

Recognition

We all want to be recognized, both for our efforts and for who we are.

Even when nurses began to organize and systematize nursing science and nursing education, it was a slow road to true recognition of their important contributions to patient care.

In the 21st century, nurses are clearly at the forefront of the healthcare industry as the largest sector of the healthcare workforce. Our contributions to patient care are irrefutable, and although the public doesn't yet fully grasp the scope of nursing practice, they recognize our importance, consistently placing their trust in us, singularly and collectively. These days, saying you're a nurse is almost like saying you're a saint. This may not be accurate, but it's how the public perceives us, for better or worse.

Among other professionals—including physicians—our standing has grown exponentially, and nursing (including Advanced Practice Nursing) is recognized widely as an intrinsic aspect of health care that will be essential to the work of caring for an aging and growing population. That said, the AMA continues to push back against expanded roles and more autonomy for APNs. In my view, those roles will need to expand due to the increasing shortage of primary care physicians.

Remuneration

When it comes to money, there are many arguments about what nurses and nursing are truly worth. In some regions of the United States, salaries have risen more visibly than in others, especially in healthcare meccas like Boston, Atlanta, and San Francisco. In places like New Mexico, where I currently reside, salaries seem somewhat stagnant.

Remuneration is important since it's actually a reflection of how we're recognized, respected, and valued. Salaries that don't rise, even with increases in the general cost of living, don't make us feel valued. With mandatory overtime and increased workloads our salaries can seem less and less attractive over time if they don't keep pace with reality.

We all want to be paid fairly for what we do. When I compare nurses to musicians, athletes, and movie stars, it doesn't make sense that those who save lives, care for the dying, and tend to the sick earn a mere fraction of what those who entertain us enjoy. Face it, The Rolling Stones' profits for one performance far exceeds what the nursing workforce of an entire hospital makes in a year.

So, we're not flashy, sexy, or well known, but we wipe bottoms, get exposed to infectious blood, and hold the hand of the dying. How much is that truly worth?

Respect

Ah, R-E-S-P-E-C-T. We've sung about it, talked about it, and demanded it. And do we have it? Some will say yes and some will say no, but it's clear that respect for nurses has risen astronomically over the decades. In Victorian times, nurses were often seen as "loose women" and "opium users" with poor morals, gallivanting with doctors when they should have been home baking cookies, feeding babies, and ministering to their husbands' needs. Now we're seen as angels and saints who (shockingly) wear teddy bear scrubs and (sadly) work double shifts on a regular basis.

As for the teddy bear scrubs, don't get me started. I've written about that subject before, and while I see their appropriateness in the pediatric ward, I don't see how teddy bears and cartoons on the Med Surg floor gain us anything but a childlike, diminutive appearance. (Picture morning rounds with the physician in a lab coat and tie, the residents in coats and nice clothes, and the nurse in scrubs covered with Sponge Bobs and hearts. I wonder who looks more professional, but that's my bias against cartoon scrubs in a unit serving adult patients. As I said, don't get me started!)

Yes, we all want respect, and we expect that it will be ours based on our education, professionalism, knowledge, and incredible nursing skills. However, respect doesn't necessarily come with the territory, but we can continue to earn it, demand it, and instill it in others by showing it to one another and ourselves.

With rampant nurse-to-nurse bullying (also known these days as "horizontal violence"), I wonder how nurses have managed to internalize so much oppression that they consistently turn on one another. This is a sad state of affairs, and I call on all nurses who want to be respected to say no to the culture of bullying. We need to stand up to bullies, call them on their bullshit, and demand that bullies be removed from practice. We can respect ourselves more if we stand up to those who disrespect us.

Be the Change

It may be cliché, but we nurses need to be the change we want to see in the world. If we want more respect and recognition, let's shower one another with respect and recognition, and then some. And if we need more for ourselves, let's ask for it.

Nursing is poised to experience huge growth and huge challenges as the aging of the population continues apace. Let's bring recognition and respect to the table, and perhaps remuneration will follow.

CHAPTER 17

Your Nursing Career: Stagnation or Flow?

A S NURSES, our careers are fed by movement, not stagnation. Nursing can be a dynamic career path, and how you approach the trajectory of your professional development can be greatly influenced by many aspects of your life. At this juncture, is your career stagnant or flowing?

When you take a look at your nursing career, is it a flowing river of possibility and growth, or is it a dry riverbed that's thirsty for the water of your curiosity?

The flow of your career is a perpetual movement if you allow it to be, and you must consistently guard against burnout and the loss of ambition and motivation.

Still Waters Run Deep

While forward movement is what we're looking for in the bigger picture, stillness can also be our ally, especially if it's stillness born of contemplative curiosity, not of complacency or fear.

Making a change in your employment out of a simple, burning need for change isn't necessarily a great strategy. It's sort of like moving across the country in search of what's frequently called a "geographic cure." The novelty may help for a while, but decisions made with more forethought and reasoning are generally recommended—and often more successful and fruitful.

If you're feeling the need for change but aren't certain what that change should be, looking inward for guidance can sometimes be more powerful than looking outward.

Being Expansive

At different times we flow like a river, sit still like a deep, cold lake, or feel expansive like the sea. That expansiveness can be where the ideas flow, and these times can be when you reach out to those who can open your mind to the possibilities that perhaps you can't see. At moments of expansion we allow our hearts and spirits to take the broader view.

When we feel stuck in our nursing career and can't seem to see the forest for the trees, we may need to prop the door open to greater possibilities.

The ocean cycles through its tides, and it never argues with what comes naturally. And for us, it's the same. Our career can hit low tide or high tide, a period of ebbing or flowing, and our success, happiness, and satisfaction depend on how much we can remain open to what's next.

Fly Free

Your nursing career should not feel restrictive. Rather, it should feel expansive and filled with possibility.

If your career is not at a place of expansion, don't despair. There are places to turn for support, people to lean on, professionals to advise you, and a deep place within you that may have all of the answers you need.

Look for the avenues that offer growth and a sense of possibility, and then lean into those places. If one street leads to a dead end, turn around and go elsewhere. The map isn't necessarily predetermined, and the outcome is up for grabs. And sometimes, when the path isn't entirely clear, we create the path by taking the first step.

You were meant to fly, not to be boxed in or pigeonholed. I wish you the flight of your life. And when you look down at that ocean or river of possibility, know that there's enough abundance for all to experience a nursing career filled with satisfaction, growth, and joy.

Enjoy the ride.

CHAPTER 18

Got Soul, Nurses?

WHAT DOES IT MEAN to have soul? Does it mean you've read *Chicken Soup for the Nurse's Soul*? Does it mean you listen and dance to James Brown? Does it mean you cook spicy food? Well, it could mean those things, but it's a whole lot more.

Having soul is allowing your soul to shine through you. It means that your soul—or spirit, if that feels better—isn't crushed by the imperatives, limitations, restrictions, and burdens of nursing. Having soul means you know who you are, what you want, where you're going, and you don't feel that your job is crushing you into oblivion, squeezing your energy until there's nothing left.

Having soul means your soul is able to survive your work and thrive beyond it. Soul means that nursing may be what you do and part of who you are, but knowing simultaneously that you're bigger than that. You're bigger than the bullies. You're bigger than the administration that wouldn't know patient or nurse satisfaction if it socked them in the eye. It means that you're bigger than it all, and that nursing doesn't define you in a way that puts you in a box from which it feels there's no escape.

Your soul—your spirit—should not be crushed by nursing and being a nurse. Your spirit should soar. And if your spirit isn't soaring, there's something wrong. Yes, we all need to earn a living and put food on the table. But if our jobs are deadening, numbing, or not feeding us on more than just the physical plane, then there's inner work to be done.

Cultivate Soul

So, how do you cultivate soul, both in your nursing work and when you come home? Well, there are many ways.

Does your work come home with you? If so, when you get home, put those scrubs in the laundry, take a shower, wash that job right out of your hair, and do something you love. Go for a walk, paint a picture, play with the dog, organize your stamp collection. Whatever it is, do what feeds your soul, lightens your spirit, and gladdens your heart.

At work, try to bring lightness. Try not to be reactive. Take things in stride. See through your colleagues' stress in order to see the light within them. See the little children inside your patients and colleagues, the children who want to have their candy, take a nap, and receive a nice pat on the head for being good. Cultivate soul in others by recognizing that their soul, like yours, also needs love and nurturing.

Make sure that, somehow, your job doesn't eat you alive. Make sure there's juice left for your life outside of nursing. In whatever ways you need to, don't allow nursing and being a nurse to consume you. Many of us have been there, and Lord knows it ain't pretty.

Human Kind

I love the bumper sticker that says, "Human kind—be both." We nurses can sometimes feel like automatons, and we need to remember our own humanity as often as we remember and recognize the humanity of others.

Do we give ourselves the human kindness that we give to others? Do we lavish upon ourselves the care that we give to our patients, friends, and families?

Be a human, embrace your humanity, treat yourself with kindness, and nurture that soul within you that's crying out for kindness.

Cultivate the grace of gentle kindness and compassion for your own soul, and decide to allow that nurse's soul to shine.

About Nurse Keith

KEITH CARLSON is a holistic career coach for nurses, award-winning nurse blogger, writer, consultant, podcaster, speaker, author, and popular career columnist. With more than two decades of nursing experience, Keith deeply understands the issues faced by 21st-century nurses. His message of savvy career management and professional satisfaction reaches tens of thousands of nurses worldwide.

Keith has written for Nurse.com, Nurse.org, Working Nurse Magazine, Multibriefs News Service, American Sentinel University, StaffGarden, and other online platforms. Keith has contributed chapters for a number of books related to the nursing profession. His first book, "Savvy Networking For Nurses: Getting Connected and Staying Connected in the 21st Century", has already helped thousands of readers sharpen their skills in personal branding and professional networking.

Based in beautiful Santa Fe, New Mexico with his lovely wife and stunningly adorable and intelligent cat, Keith enjoys time with elders, children, animals, and the occasional adult.

How to Find Keith

Website: NurseKeith.com
Blog: DigitalDoorway.blogspot.com
Podcast: NurseKeithShow.libsyn.com
Facebook.com/nursekeithcoaching
Twitter.com/nursekeith
Instagram.com/nursekeithcoaching
LinkedIn.com/in/KeithAllanCarlson

Notes

Notes

Notes

Notes

60254470R00060

Made in the USA
Middletown, DE
27 December 2017